Viewpoints

A Guide to Conflict Resolution and Decision Making for Adolescents

Nancy G. Guerra ▼ Ann Moore ▲ Ronald G. Slaby

Research Press   2612 North Mattis Avenue   Champaign, Illinois 61821

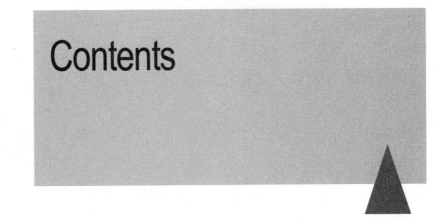

Contents

Using This Manual

This manual is about understanding yourself and others (and their points of view) and about confronting common problems and solving them effectively.

Problems are part of everyone's life. There is *no one* in the world who has never had problems to solve. Problems can be simple or complex, but they are a part of life, and *you* can solve those within your control.

You can go through this manual on your own or in small group. If you are working in a group, be sure to follow the Six Skills for Group Members:

LISTENING

When someone is talking, listen to what he or she is saying. Please do not interrupt in the middle of a sentence. Pay attention to what the person is saying—not what you'll say next.

SUMMARIZING AND RESTATING

To show you have been listening, try to begin your reply by summarizing and restating what the other person has said.

RESPECT

While you may not agree with other group members, you should respect their right to their own opinions, thoughts, and feelings.

OPENNESS AND HONESTY

While only you know what you're willing to discuss in the group, be sure that when you do discuss something, you say what's really on your mind and tell the truth.

SENSITIVITY

If you don't agree with what someone says or does, let that person know without being overly critical. Also remember to let someone know when you do agree with what he or she says.

CONFIDENTIALITY

Experiences group members share about (or discuss) should not be discussed with anyone once the session is over.

Thinking about Our Problems

Introduction

A problem is a situation that calls for change, a solution, an answer. There are many different types of personal problems. Some problems are relatively simple: deciding what to wear to a party, whether to study for a test or go out with friends, and so on. Some problems are harder to solve, particularly when they involve other people: deciding which of two friends to invite to a concert, trying to resolve a conflict with one's supervisor, and so on.

Do you know anyone who has *never* been faced with a personal problem? You may know some people who have failed to solve their problems and others who have thought of successful solutions. But chances are you have never met anyone who is completely problem-free. It is important for you to realize that problems are a *normal* part of any person's life, and that, as a part of life, problems can be solved. Most of the problems you encounter can be solved effectively.

In this lesson, you will have a chance to think about different problems people might confront. Two specific problems will be presented, one involving a parent-child conflict and one involving a difficult situation between two friends.

You will then review Eight Steps to Personal Success—a method of problem solving that has proven successful for others. Following these steps can help you to be more in control of your life and get along better with others. You can strengthen your problem-solving abilities with practice. Practice will build your confidence. The idea is to meet each challenge, use your new skills, and build one success upon another. Success is fun. Therefore, believe it or not, problem solving can be fun!

Rita often spent hours in her bedroom by herself. She would often just lie on her bed and stare at the ceiling, thinking about how hard it had been for her to make friends in high school. "Why don't the other girls like me?" she wondered. "Why doesn't someone give me a break? It must be because I'm poor and I don't have nice clothes or nice things like everyone else. If only I were rich, I wouldn't have any more problems. If only I were rich . . ."

1. Do you agree with Rita's thinking? Will her thinking help her solve her problems? Why?

_____

_____

2. Sometimes you might think that people never have any problems if they are rich, smart, beautiful, or famous. But can anyone ever be completely free of problems? Why?

_____

_____

3. What are some problems that each of the following people might have?

a. A beautiful and successful 38-year-old movie actress

_____

_____

b. A 60-year-old prison guard

_____

_____

c. A 3-year-old girl with eight brothers and sisters

_____

_____

d. A 16-year-old boy from a very wealthy family who has
   just been sent to live at boarding school

_____

_____

e. A young woman who has just been the victim of a violent crime

_____

_____

f. A United States senator who has been in office 3 years

_____

_____

g. A 25-year-old teacher

_____

_____

4. Now take some _time to think._ Have you ever had a difficult
   problem to solve? Were you able to solve it? How? (If not,
   describe a solution that might have worked.)

_____

_____

_____

_____

It's important for you to realize that everyone at one time or another faces a variety of problems and that usually these problems can be solved effectively.

Patty's Dilemma

Patty was in the 10th grade at Valley High. She had always been a good athlete and was really excited when the coach asked her to play on the varsity baseball team. She used to throw the ball and practice batting almost every Sunday with her dad. But now that her parents were divorced and she lived with her mom, she hardly spent any time with her dad.

Patty's father had played baseball in the minor leagues. "Boy," Patty thought, "will he ever be proud of me now!" But when she went home to tell her mother the good news, things did not turn out as she had expected.

"No daughter of mine is going to play varsity baseball," her mother said flatly.

"But, Mom," she said, "Please let me have a chance to play. Dad will be so proud of me! You know I've always wanted to play baseball. Please, Mom, just this once."

"I just don't even want to discuss it," said her mother. "You're NOT going to play."

The next day when Patty went to school, she tried to avoid the coach. She spent a lot of time thinking about what she could do. As she came out of her last class, she ran into the coach.

"Well, Patty," said the coach, "You're going to be a great player. I'll see you tomorrow at practice."

1. Why do you think Patty's mother doesn't want her to play baseball?

_____

_____

_____

2. Do you think any of these reasons are good reasons? Which ones?

_____

_____

_____

3. What's the most important issue? *(Check one only.)*

   ☐ Patty may not get to play.

   ☐ Patty is being treated unfairly because she's a girl.

   ☐ Patty won't look good in the coach's eyes.

   ☐ Patty's mother is treating her like a baby.

4. Patty is probably angry. What might be some reasons for her to be angry with:

a. Her mother _____

_____

_____

b. Her father _____

_____

_____

c. Herself _____

_____

_____

5. What are some possible *solutions* that might help Patty with this dilemma? What advice would you give her?

_____

_____

_____

David Wilson and Tom Smith had been friends since they were in the 6th grade. They had had many good times together in high school, and they usually stayed out of trouble. But in the 12th grade, Tom began to hang around with a group of kids who used a lot of drugs. Pretty soon he started selling cocaine to some junior high school kids. When David saw how much money Tom was making, he asked Tom to let him in on a few deals.

Soon David was dealing drugs. He was really afraid he would be busted. He mentioned that both Tom and he were 18 years old and could go to prison. Tom just said they probably would never get caught, and even if they did, they could still rely on each other in prison.

But the worst happened, and David and Tom were arrested for selling cocaine to minors. They were both shocked when they were sentenced to 7 years in prison. "Well," David thought, "at least I can rely on Tom in prison." He was scared at the thought of being locked up.

The first day in prison David was approached by three black men. They told David that since he was black they did not want him to hang around with any white boys. One said, "Look, man, here the blacks stick together. The whites stick together. The Mexicans stick together. And the Indians stick together. I mean, you've gotta stick with your race."

Since Tom was white, David knew he would be in for a lot of trouble if he stayed in close contact with him. He decided that the most important thing was to survive. So he told Tom that they had better go their separate ways. Although he missed Tom, David got along fairly well with his new black friends.

One day there was a big fight out in the prison yard. When David walked over to take a closer look, he saw a white man being brutally beaten by two black men. "Poor guy," he thought. As he started to walk away he noticed that the white man was his friend, Tom.

"Hey, get off him," David said to the black guys. "He's a friend of mine."

"No one who's white is your friend," someone shouted.

"But you're going to kill him!" yelled David.

1. Why is this a difficult problem for David?

_____

_____

_____

_____

2. What is most important for David to consider? (Check one only.)

☐ David has to look out for his own safety.

☐ David should be loyal to his friend.

☐ David should stick with people of his race.

3. What should David do? Why?

_____

_____

_____

_____

Eight Steps to Personal Success

Thinking of solutions is an important part of problem solving. But there are also other things to consider. In this manual, you will learn Eight Steps to Personal Success—a method of problem solving that has proven successful for others. These steps can work for you, too.

Briefly review the eight steps. They will be discussed in detail in the rest of this manual.

1. Is there a problem?
2. Stop and think
3. Why is there a conflict?
4. What do I want?
5. Think of solutions
6. Look at consequences
7. Choose what to do and do it
8. Evaluate results

Is There a Problem? (Step 1)

Introduction

In order to solve a problem, you must first be able to decide when, in fact, you have a problem. But sometimes this is hard to determine. How do you know when you are faced with a problem? Problems often involve such things as choices, decisions, actions, goals, and consequences. You can ask yourself questions such as the following: Do I have a choice? What do I want? What do others want? Am I breaking a rule or law? Could anyone get hurt?

In this chapter, you will be asked to think about the times in your life when you are most likely to experience problems—namely, when you are under a lot of *stress*. You will also learn about deciding when a problem first occurs, as well as identifying feelings and thoughts that often let you know when a problem begins.

Before learning how to identify specific problems, think about times in your life when you might be likely to experience the most problems. This often happens when the events in your life are unusually stressful. A variety of events can cause stress for you and others.

Using the following scale, check each event that has happened to you in the past 12 months, then total your score.

Event	Value	
Divorce	73	_____
Jail term	63	_____
Death of a close family member	63	_____
Personal injury or illness	53	_____
Marriage	50	_____
Being fired from work	47	_____
Marital reconciliation in family	45	_____
Retirement	45	_____
Change in family member's health	44	_____
Pregnancy	40	_____
Sex difficulties	39	_____
Addition to family	39	_____
Change in job	39	_____
Change in earnings	38	_____
Death of a close friend	37	_____
Change of career/type of job	36	_____
Debt of over $10,000	31	_____
Change in job responsibilities	29	_____
Outstanding personal achievement	28	_____
Change in personal habits	24	_____
Trouble with boss or teacher(s)	23	_____
Change in work/school hours or conditions	20	_____
Change in residence	20	_____
Change in schools	20	_____
Change in recreational activities	20	_____
Change in church activities	19	_____
Change in social life	18	_____

Event	Value	
Loan under $10,000	17	————
Change in sleeping habits	16	————
Change in number of family gatherings	15	————
Change in eating habits	15	————
Vacation	13	————
Christmas season	12	————
Minor violation of the law	11	————
TOTAL		————

YOUR SCORE

50 or less — Things are going smoothly right now.

50–125 — Take time to relax—things are a little rough.

125–200 — Medium level of stress. At 150 you have a 50–50 chance of getting sick in the near future.

200–300 — Better take it easy. At 300 you have a 90% chance of getting sick soon.

Over 300 — Get help from friends, family, or others in coping with stress right now!

One way to reduce the stress caused by difficult situations is to identify a problem when it *first occurs* and not wait until a little problem has turned into a big one. Unfortunately, people often respond before they have defined the problem and before they have thought of a good solution.

Read each of the following examples. Check the answer that tells you when the problem began.

1. John drove home from a party after drinking 10 cans of beer. He ran over a little girl. The girl was rushed to the hospital but died a few hours later. The police came and arrested John.

    When did John's problem begin?

    ☐ When he drank 10 cans of beer

    ☐ When he got in his car after drinking too much

    ☐ When he ran over the girl

    ☐ When the girl died

    ☐ When the police came and arrested him

2. It was Tuesday night, and Alexa had her math final on Wednesday. She hadn't studied yet, so she decided she would stay up late Tuesday night and study a lot. Her friend, Marsha, called and asked her to go out to a friend's house. Alexa went with Marsha, and by the time she got home it was too late to study. Alexa failed her math test and failed the class.

    When did Alexa's problem begin?

    ☐ When she left her studying to the last minute

    ☐ When she decided to go with Marsha

    ☐ When she got home late

    ☐ When she failed the test

    ☐ When she failed the class

3. Mark had always wanted to ask Sandy out on a date. He finally got up the nerve and asked her out for Saturday night. Sandy didn't really like Mark but accepted because she had nothing else to do. But on Thursday, Bill, a boy she really liked, asked her out for Saturday. She agreed to go and forgot to tell Mark. At 7:00 P.M. on Saturday night, Mark and Bill both knocked at her door. When they realized she had made dates with both of them, they both turned and left.

When did Sandy's problem begin?

- ☐ When she accepted a date with Mark when she didn't really like him
- ☐ When she accepted a date with Bill
- ☐ When she forgot to tell Mark that she couldn't go
- ☐ When she opened the door

4. Tyrone occasionally used cocaine but did not consider himself a heavy drug user and never sold drugs. One day he met a really nice lady who seemed to be interested in him. After talking for a while, she asked him if he could buy some cocaine for her. Since he wanted to impress her, he found someone who sold him some cocaine. When he brought it to his new lady friend, she told him she was an undercover police officer and arrested him.

When did Tyrone's problem begin?

- ☐ When he started using drugs
- ☐ When he met the lady
- ☐ When he decided to get the cocaine
- ☐ When the lady turned out to be a police officer and arrested him

In each of these situations, the problem did not begin when the person was caught. Rather, it began when the person chose to do something with potentially harmful consequences.

Go back and check your answers. Did you identify correctly when the problem really began?

Write about an experience you have had when you were caught doing something wrong. You can use a minor incident, such as taking a cookie when you were told not to, or a major event, such as being arrested for a crime.

What I did was:

_____

_____

_____

_____

The first point when my problem started was:

_____

_____

_____

_____

Early Warning Signs

Your *thoughts* and *feelings* can signal that a problem is about to begin.

Thoughts	**Feelings**
Ideas from your mind, ways you understand or reason about things	Emotions, gut-level reactions (sometimes hard to control)

Stress and anxiety are *feelings* you might have when faced with problems. These feelings usually produce certain body changes that help identify anxiety. These can include the following:

Sweating	Tense muscles	Increased heart rate
Stomachache	Red face	Clenched jaw
Rapid breathing	Headache	

These are *physical reactions* to stress. These responses are similar to the reactions you have to a heavy physical workout. However, when they result from internal emotional stress, they usually feel unpleasant and produce further anxiety.

Describe a stressful situation that brought on these responses.

_____

_____

_____

_____

What were some specific physical reactions you had?

_____

_____

_____

_____

Some of the thoughts that may go with body changes are impulsive, or "hot-headed" thoughts, such as the following:

> What do I do now?
>
> I better get away fast.
>
> It doesn't matter anyway.
>
> I'm going to hurt him/her.
>
> I can get away.
>
> Now I'm really in trouble.

These hot-headed thoughts often involve *fight or flight responses*, such as "I'm going to hurt him/her" (a fight response) or "I can get away" (a flight response). These thoughts may also come from a "no-win" position, such as "It doesn't matter anyway."

Have you ever had any hot-headed thoughts? If so, write them below.

1. _____

2. _____

3. _____

4. _____

"Cool-headed" thoughts are alternative statements you can use to help you stay calm and better solve the problem confronting you.

Read each of the following cool-headed thoughts aloud.

> Stay calm—don't get too upset.
>
> I can work out a plan.
>
> What is it I have to do?
>
> I know how to control my anger.

There is no need for a fight.

Don't worry—it won't help anything.

I really can't afford to get in trouble.

Next write down some of your own favorite cool-headed responses to a problem situation.

1. _____

2. _____

3. _____

4. _____

Practice one (or more) of these cool-headed responses next time you are in a stressful situation.

Stop and Think (Step 2)

Introduction

The next important step in effective problem solving is learning to *stop and think* before acting. Doing this allows you to control your emotions and to think calmly. Deliberate, rational thought takes place only when you "cool down" after a difficult confrontation.

You may be tempted to deal with these situations with *hot-headed thoughts*, such as "I'm going to hit him" or "I've got to run." Remember to try to use *cool-headed thoughts*, such as "I can work out a plan." It takes practice to put off the emotional, or hot-headed, reaction. But delaying a response is important in order to maintain control and to achieve what you really want in any stressful situation. Otherwise, you allow your emotions to rule your responses, and then almost anything can happen! So, to stay in control, be sure to wait a moment, collect your thoughts, and be cool under pressure.

A woman was waiting at a bus stop when a little lizard jumped on her foot and scurried up her leg. She screamed, jumped to her feet, and proceeded to shake the lizard out of the leg of her pants. Her frantic motions attracted the attention of a young man, who immediately assumed that the woman was having a convulsion. He grabbed her and tried to force a pencil between her teeth to keep her from biting her tongue.* Another bystander, assuming that the first man was attacking the woman, came to her rescue and tried to drive the first man off. In the middle of all the commotion, the police arrived.

*This is NOT the correct thing to do if someone has a convulsion or seizure.

Who were all the people who didn't *stop and think*?

_____

_____

_____

_____

In order to solve problems effectively, you must be able to think calmly and not act on impulse. Many situations are really quite different than they first seem to be. That's why it's so important not to respond immediately (unless, of course, you are faced with danger and must act quickly).

There are many different ways you can give yourself time to cool down and think things through carefully:

Silently count to 10 (or 20 if necessary).

Take five deep breaths.

Think of something that makes you happy.

Recognize that you may be in a bad mood and stay away from potential problems or situations. Tell yourself you'll feel different later.

Think of the consequences of certain acts.

Think of your future goals.

Any other suggestions?

_____

_____

What technique will work best for you?

_____

_____

Try the technique you think will work best for you at least once in the next week. Then come back to this page and describe the situation and how you handled it.

_____

_____

_____

_____

_____

_____

_____

_____

If you take time to *stop and think* when you have a problem, you can become more aware of your reactions and practice cool-headed thinking. In the following situations, the main character is faced with a problem.

Answer the questions that follow based on what you have learned from this manual.

1. Michael is on his way to class. He knows he can't be late. A boy he doesn't know is walking the other way. When the boy passes by, he makes an insulting remark to Michael.

a. How do you think Michael *feels*?

_____

_____

b. What *physical reactions* is Michael probably having?

_____

_____

c. What *hot-headed thoughts* might he be having?

_____

_____

d. What would he be likely to do if he responded *immediately*?

_____

_____

e. What *technique* can he practice to give himself time to *stop and think*?

_____

_____

f. What would be some *cool-headed thoughts* he could practice?

_____

_____

2. Marta, a 16-year-old girl, is driving by herself on the freeway one
   Friday night. Her car runs out of gas, and she pulls off the road.
   She panics and doesn't know what to do. In a few minutes, an
   older man in an expensive new car pulls over and asks if she
   wants a ride.

a. How do you think Marta *feels*?

_____

_____

b. What *physical reactions* is Marta probably having?

_____

_____

c. What *hot-headed thoughts* might she be having?

_____

_____

d. What would she be likely to do if she responded *immediately*?

_____

_____

e. What *technique* can she practice to give herself time to
   stop and think?

_____

_____

f. What would be some *cool-headed thoughts* she could practice?

_____

_____

3. Jerry is working in a discount stereo store. An old friend who has done him a few big favors comes into the store. He buys a blank tape, and Jerry puts it in a bag. A few minutes later, the friend hands Jerry a small walkie talkie set and says, "Here, Jerry, pretend to ring this up and put it in my bag. Hurry up—your boss is in the storeroom."

a. How do you think Jerry *feels*?

_____

_____

b. What *physical reactions* is Jerry probably having?

_____

_____

c. What *hot-headed thoughts* might he be having?

_____

_____

d. What would he be likely to do if he responded *immediately*?

_____

_____

e. What *technique* can he practice to give himself time to *stop and think*?

_____

_____

f. What would be some *cool-headed thoughts* he could practice?

_____

_____

4. Andrea has finally decided to go on a diet. She has lost 6 pounds in 2 weeks. But today she is feeling a little depressed. Her mouth starts to water when she sees the gooey fudge brownies for dessert. "Go on, eat it," says her friend.

a. How do you think Andrea *feels*?

_____

_____

b. What *physical reactions* is Andrea probably having?

_____

_____

c. What *hot-headed thoughts* might she be having?

_____

_____

d. What would she be likely to do if she responded *immediately*?

_____

_____

e. What *technique* can she practice to give herself time to *stop and think*?

_____

_____

f. What would be some *cool-headed thoughts* she could practice?

_____

_____

Lesson 4 | # Why Is There a Conflict? Get the Facts/Check My Beliefs (Step 3)

Introduction

An important part of accurately identifying a problem is getting enough information about it. For example, in order to decide if you have enough money to buy something, you must know how much the item costs. If you are going to buy something on credit, you need to know what the monthly payments will be and how much money you will need to earn in order to make the payments.

However, in everyday life people often make judgments or take actions without really knowing enough about the situation. For instance, how long after you've met a new person do you decide if you like him or her? One minute? Five minutes? Two hours? On which of the following characteristics do you base your judgment?

Check those that apply.

☐ Is the person good looking?

☐ Is the person clean or dirty?

☐ Does the person wear nice clothes?

☐ Does the person have a funny voice?

☐ Does the person laugh at the wrong time?

☐ Is the person the same race as I am?

☐ Does the person have any strange habits?

☐ Have I heard any rumors about the person?

Other characteristics I judge people by:

_____

_____

_____

_____

_____

One way you might make an error in judgment is by not getting enough information before making that judgment.

Another important consideration is any *preconceived biases* that can affect or limit the information you seek. A *bias* is a tendency to be for or against something prior to getting the specific facts. It is like a filter on a pair of glasses. The filter can distort your view in many ways—you can jump to the wrong conclusion before you get the facts.

Biases often occur when you take one specific example and generalize it to cover all similar situations. For example, if a person with red hair hits you, you could develop a bias against all people with red hair. Biases often interfere with effective problem solving because they prevent you from being open-minded.

In this lesson, you will first review the importance of getting the facts when you are faced with a problem situation. Then you will be asked to critically examine some biases that may affect your definition of a problem. The role of *prejudice* in personal decision making will also be discussed.

In each of the following situations, a wide variety of things could be going on. In the space provided, write down two possible explanations. Then write down whatever additional information you would need.

1. Your girlfriend (boyfriend) is standing very close and talking to a boy (girl) you've never seen before.

Possible explanations:

a. _____

_____

_____

b. _____

_____

_____

Further information needed to come to a conclusion:

_____

_____

2. Someone in a car behind you keeps honking the horn.

Possible explanations:

a. _____

_____

_____

b. _____

_____

_____

Further information needed to come to a conclusion:

_____

_____

3. A boy or girl next to you spits on the ground near you.

Possible explanations:

a. _____

_____

_____

b. _____

_____

_____

Further information needed to come to a conclusion:

_____

_____

4. Your girlfriend or boyfriend is 2 hours late for a date.

Possible explanations:

a. _____

_____

_____

b. _____

_____

_____

Further information needed to come to a conclusion:

_____

_____

5. A person you don't like makes a face as he or she walks by you.

Possible explanations:

a. _____

_____

_____

b. _____

_____

_____

Further information needed to come to a conclusion:

_____

_____

As you can see, there are many different possibilities for each situation—what is needed is more information. Someone may make a face because he or she is intentionally giving you a dirty look, *or* that person may just be angry about something that has nothing to do with you. It is always important to get all the facts in a situation before coming to any conclusions.

Write about a situation you've been in where you made a judgment and found out later that you were mistaken.

_____

_____

_____

_____

_____

It is easy to make quick judgments about what people are like when you don't know them well. To some extent, everyone does this. But a person may have several different sides to his or her personality. It is important to remember not to judge another person too quickly. Your beliefs and biases might be influencing you.

The following are true statements made by different people about two actual men. Read each set of statements and answer the questions that follow.

TED

He was a nice guy.

He had very few friends in high school, but his interest in athletics and his handsome features enabled him to have his share of girls.

He was always talking about psychology.

He spent 2 years trying to save lives as an ambulance technician.

He liked to watch television, especially situation comedies and police shows.

He hated the idea of hitting an animal with a car, and he carefully watched out for them when he was driving.

1. What are some things Ted might like to do?

_____

_____

_____

2. What occupation might he choose?

_____

_____

_____

3. Would you like to be friends with Ted? Why?

_____

_____

_____

AL

His parents were afraid he was below normal in intelligence.

His teacher told his father, "He will never make a success of anything."

He loved music and played the violin, but he wasn't very good at it.

He liked mathematics, and his ideas were often far beyond what anyone else could understand.

He often went around in an old suit with baggy trousers.

He told a young woman he knew, "I'm not much of a family man."

1. What are some things Al might like to do?

_____

_____

_____

2. What occupation might he choose?

_____

_____

_____

3. Would you like to be friends with Al? Why?

_____

_____

_____

Turn the page upside-down to find out more about Ted and Al. After reading the information, think about the basis upon which you made your judgments about Ted and Al. Did your biases affect your judgments? Did you need more information?

Ted is Ted Bundy, convicted of brutally killing more than a dozen young women over the course of 2 years. Al is Albert Einstein, a scientist known throughout the world for his brilliant mind and his efforts to promote world peace.

A Biased View

Read each of the following statements, indicating your agreement or disagreement by marking "T" (True) or "F" (False) in the space to the left. Regardless of your choice, make a case for why each statement is false.

_____ 1. A lot of people in this world are mean.

_____

_____

_____

_____ 2. Certain groups of people are inferior to other groups.

_____

_____

_____

_____ 3. If someone is different from my race, I consider that person to be an enemy.

_____

_____

_____

_____ 4. If someone looks at me the wrong way, that person is asking for trouble.

_____

_____

_____

_____ 5. Everyone I know is always ready to fight.

_____

_____

_____

_____ 6. Poor people don't want to work. That's why they're poor.

_____

_____

_____

_____ 7. Teachers only give you bad grades when they don't like kids.

_____

_____

_____

_____ 8. Guys should take advantage of girls if they can.

_____

_____

_____

_____ 9. Some people are asking to be hurt.

_____

_____

_____

_____10. Some people deserve to be killed.

_____

_____

_____

_____11. Only cowards refuse to fight.

_____

_____

_____

_____12. People pretend to care, but they really always want
           something for themselves.

_____

_____

_____

Prejudice is a type of bias that involves a preformed judgment about someone or something. Prejudice is unreasonable because it is not based on fact. It is usually negative, or against a person or group of people.

Do you make judgments about people based on the way they look, their race, their age, and so on? Giving your true feelings in each case, read the list below and answer the questions that follow.

Person A: A male gang member

Person B: A cheerful cocktail waitress

Person C: A young teacher

Person D: A wealthy rock star

Person E: An old business executive who chain smokes

Person F: A teenage mother of twins

Person G: An ex-convict with 10 prior felony convictions

Person H: A stunningly beautiful woman

Person I: A medically trained heroine user

Person J: A middle-aged female police officer

Person K: A black high school principal

Person L: A hard-working field hand

1. Would you lend money to Person G?

_____

To Person C? _____

2. If you had a successful business, would you hire Person I?

_____

Person F? _____

3. If you were a parent, would you let Person A baby-sit for your children?

_____

Person E? _____

4. Would you choose Person D to be on your winning softball team?

_____

Person H? _____

5. If you had to understand a difficult math problem in order to graduate from high school, would you seek help from Person K?

_____

Person D? _____

6. If you were stuck in an elevator, would you want to have Person J with you?

_____

Person L? _____

7. If you were a police officer and a crime had been committed, would you be likely to question Person B?

_____

Person G? _____

All of us have experienced some form of prejudice, whether we are aware of it or not. Do you think some people might be prejudiced against you? Explain why.

_____

_____

_____

_____

Why Is There a Conflict? The Other's Perspective (Step 3)

Introduction

Dear A.B.:

I'm a teenage boy with a big problem. There's a really cool girl at school named Dolores. I really want to meet her. But I'm so shy, every time I see her, I just look the other way. She must think I'm a jerk. I probably shouldn't bother trying to meet her. What do you think?

—Joe

Dear A.B.:

I'm a teenage girl with a big problem. There's a guy named Joe I really like, but he just ignores me. I always sit near him at lunch, but whenever I look at him he just looks the other way. He must think I'm a real loser. Why do you think he doesn't like me? What should I do?

—Dolores

As you can see in this example, Dolores and Joe have different ideas of what is going on. Dolores things Joe doesn't like her because he thinks she's a loser, while Joe thinks he looks like a jerk to Dolores.

When confronting the same situation, two people often see things very differently. That is because everyone is *unique* and sees and interprets events according to his or her own *perspective* or *point of view*. One of the most difficult tasks in effective problem solving is to understand the perspective or point of view of everyone involved.

Read each of the following situations. Then write a few sentences describing how each person involved probably views the situation— that is, his or her *perspective* or *point of view*. (If you are working in a small group, try role-playing one of the roles, switching roles, and then discussing your perspective in each role.)

SITUATION 1

Tanya, an 8-year-old girl, comes home from school every day and must wait alone until her mother arrives from work. Her mother, Mrs. C., is single, works very hard at a low-paying job, and is exhausted when she gets home.

One day, Tanya decides to surprise her mother by preparing a spaghetti dinner. She gets out a big pot and pours in some tomato sauce. She turns the flame up high so her sauce will be well-cooked. In a frying pan, she starts browning some meat.

But the phone rings, and Tanya rushes to the bedroom to answer it, forgetting to turn off the stove. She talks to her friend for a few minutes, then goes back to the kitchen to finish cooking dinner. But dinner is already ruined, and so is the kitchen ceiling, wallpaper, and floor— there is tomato sauce and grease splattered everywhere. As Tanya hurriedly tries to clean up the mess, her mother comes home from work. When she sees the kitchen, she lets out a loud scream.

a. Describe this situation from Tanya's point of view.

_____

_____

_____

b. Describe this situation from her mother's point of view.

_____

_____

_____

SITUATION 2

Rob and his friends are invited to a party. Michele, a girl that Rob really likes, will be there, and Rob is excited. As he's getting ready to go, his mother asks him to clean up his room first. But Rob's friends are coming by in a few minutes, and he doesn't have time. He tells his mom to leave him alone. He says he'll clean his room later. His mom doesn't like his response and tells him that now he can't go to the party.

a. Describe this situation from Rob's point of view.

_____

_____

_____

b. Describe this situation from his mom's point of view.

_____

_____

_____

SITUATION 3

Now think of a problem you have had with another person. Tell what the problem was about.

_____

_____

_____

_____

_____

_____

_____

_____

a. Describe the problem from your point of view.

_____

_____

_____

_____

_____

b. Describe the problem from the other person's point of view.

_____

_____

_____

_____

_____

The following scenario was observed by eight different people, each with his or her own perspective or point of view.

Silver Spur Shopping Mall was a popular place for teenagers. Most of them just window-shopped, got something to eat, and went home. But lately some really rowdy kids had started hanging around and getting into some occasional fights.

One day, Randy W. was looking at some earrings for his girlfriend at Miller's Gems. All of a sudden, David S. grabbed his arm and started to beat him up.

A crowd quickly gathered. Each person in the crowd had a slightly different perspective, or point of view.

Write down what you think would be the perspective (point of view) of each of the following people.

1. Mr. Miller (store owner):

_____

_____

_____

2. Cindy W. (Randy's mother):

_____

_____

_____

3. Medical doctor (who happened to be walking by):

_____

_____

_____

4. Arnie L. (David's brother):

_____

_____

_____

5. Police officer (called to the scene):

_____

_____

_____

6. Sugar Babe Bobson (professional fighter, also shopping):

_____

_____

_____

7. You (you happen to be out shopping that day):

_____

_____

_____

Now finish the following statement.

Everyone is unique and sees things differently because:

_____

_____

_____

_____

Problem Situations (Review)

Introduction

In the previous lessons, you learned the first three steps to effective problem solving:

1. Is there a problem?

2. Stop and think

3. Why is there a conflict?

Now it's your turn to see if you can apply these skills to problem situations. You will recall that first you need to recognize when a problem really exists. You will need to tune in to your feelings and look inside to be aware of your responses. (Remember, physical reactions are body changes you experience under stress. These include sweating, tense muscles, headache, increased heart rate, rapid breathing, and others.)

Then you will need to assess the mood you were in *before* the problem began to see if that state of mind is influencing your reactions. In addition, you will want to practice the automatic response of stopping to think before taking action.

It is also important to gather all the information about a situation before you react. In addition, you will want to be sure that your information is accurate. This way, you will avoid jumping to the wrong conclusion about what is happening. You might try thinking about a time when you faced a problem and you lost your temper or overreacted in the heat of the moment—only to find out you were mistaken about the facts. How embarrassing! So be sure to gather *all* the information and then proceed to check that information against your beliefs and biases. Apply all of these skills to the situations in this chapter.

SITUATION 1: DON AND KESHIA

Don and Keshia had a date at 7:00 P.M. to go to a concert. Keshia went shopping with her friends but left early to be sure she was home on time. Don really liked Keshia a lot and was looking forward to going to the concert. He didn't want to do anything to make her mad. Before he went to pick her up, he stopped by a friend's house and had a few cans of beer. Soon he realized that it was already 6:45 P.M. He quickly started to leave. But his friend got mad and said, "Hey, we're still partying. Don't let some girl tell you where to go!" Don wasn't sure what to do.

1. Do you think Don *knows* he has a problem?　　☐ Yes　☐ No

2. How do you think Don *feels*?

_____

_____

3. What *physical reactions* might he be having?

_____

_____

4. Should Don take time to *stop and think*?　　☐ Yes　☐ No

5. What do you think Don is *saying* to himself?

_____

_____

6. Does Don need any more *information*? If he does, what does he need to know?

_____

_____

7. Write a clear *definition* of Don's problem.

_____

_____

_____

_____

Don decided to stay with his friend. By the time he got to Keshia's house it was 9:00 P.M. Keshia was furious when she answered the door.

1. Do you think Keshia *knows* she has a problem? ☐ Yes ☐ No

2. How do you think Keshia *feels*?

_____

_____

3. What *physical reactions* might she be having?

_____

_____

4. Should Keshia take time to *stop and think*? ☐ Yes ☐ No

5. What do you think Keshia is *saying* to herself?

_____

_____

6. Does Keshia need any more *information*? If she does, what information does she need?

_____

_____

7. Write a clear *definition* of Keshia's problem.

_____

_____

_____

_____

SITUATION 2: OSCAR AND RAMON

Oscar is going to his class. Things haven't been going too well for him, and he is in a bad mood. Ramon walks by, frowns at Oscar, and mutters something. Oscar is sure it's an insult to him.

1. Do you think Oscar *knows* he has a problem?   ☐ Yes   ☐ No

2. How do you think Oscar *feels*?

_____

_____

3. What *physical reactions* might he be having?

_____

_____

4. Should Oscar take time to *stop and think*?   ☐ Yes   ☐ No

5. What do you think Oscar is *saying* to himself?

_____

_____

6. Does Oscar need any more *information*? If so, what does he need to know?

_____

_____

7. Write a clear *definition* of Oscar's problem.

_____

_____

_____

_____

SITUATION 3: RHONDA AND THE BABYSITTER

Rhonda is 9 years old. She has always been very close to her father. Since her parents divorced, she has lived with him. However, he is very busy and frequently leaves her with an adult babysitter named Rick. Soon Rick begins touching her in ways that make her feel uncomfortable. She wishes her father wouldn't leave her alone with Rick. One night, Rick sits down on her bed and tells Rhonda that if she likes him, she will be "nice" to him.

1. Do you think Rhonda *knows* she has a problem? ☐ Yes ☐ No

2. How do you think Rhonda *feels*?

_____

_____

3. What *physical reactions* might she be having?

_____

_____

4. Should Rhonda take time to *stop and think*? ☐ Yes ☐ No

5. What do you think Rhonda is *saying* to herself?

_____

_____

6. Does Rhonda need any more *information*? If so, what does she need to know?

_____

_____

7. Write a clear *definition* of Rhonda's problem.

_____

_____

_____

_____

What Do I Want? (Step 4)

In order to solve problems effectively, you must first know what you want. This is your *goal*. In this chapter, you will learn about different types of goals:

1. Basic goals

2. Action goals

3. Short-term goals

4. Long-term goals

It is important to decide whether your goals are realistic or unrealistic. Often this decision depends on your own personal strengths and weaknesses. For instance, it would be unrealistic for a very short person to try out for professional basketball. But this does not mean that it is impossible to overcome limitations such as this—in some cases goals like this have been achieved by persevering (not giving up).

What you want to achieve is a certain balance in your life. This way, you weigh your ambitions (and even your wildest dreams) against your real talents and capabilities. However, keep in mind that hard work and determination can count greatly in getting ahead. Therefore, be certain not to limit your vision of what you want to become. Simply try to be honest with yourself and be willing to strive to meet your goals, no matter what they may be. Then work on maintaining a positive outlook and remember to reassess your goals now and then.

Basic goals are broad goals for your personal well-being—they are the ultimate goals for your actions. While there is no prescribed list of basic goals, they could include the following:

1. To be respected by others
2. To achieve something important
3. To be loved by others
4. To help others
5. To be free of pain or suffering
6. To be successful at things you do
7. To look your best
8. To enjoy yourself

What are five *basic goals* that are important to you? List them.

1. _____

2. _____

3. _____

4. _____

5. _____

Action goals represent specific acts or steps you take to meet your basic goals. For example, getting an "A" on a test is an *action goal*—the *basic goal* is to be successful.

Each of the following are action goals. List some basic goals they represent.

1. To eat low-calorie foods
   Basic goals:

   _____

   _____

2. To get a high-paying job
   Basic goals:

   _____

   _____

3. To have children
   Basic goals:

   _____

   _____

4. To look tough
   Basic goals:

   _____

   _____

5. To go on a 2-week vacation
   Basic goals:

   _____

   _____

In the examples just given, you may have listed the same basic goals for some of the different action goals. Your basic goals are probably both realistic and necessary. However, your action goals may be any of the following:

    1. Totally unrealistic

    2. Realistic but difficult to accomplish

    3. Relatively easy for you to accomplish

In setting your action goals, it is a good idea to have some realistic but difficult goals as well as some relatively easy goals.

Realistic and Unrealistic Goals

Read the following statements, indicating whether you think the action goals are unrealistic, realistic but difficult, or easy to accomplish.

1. A convicted murderer, who is serving life in prison without parole, wants to go home for the Christmas holidays.

   Unrealistic ☐   Realistic ☐   Easy ☐

2. An unattractive, overweight boy with a great sense of humor wants to become a movie star.

   Unrealistic ☐   Realistic ☐   Easy ☐

3. A 16-year-old girl who has always had poor grades in school wants to become a medical doctor.

   Unrealistic ☐   Realistic ☐   Easy ☐

4. An 18-year-old boy who is very short wants to play professional basketball.

   Unrealistic ☐   Realistic ☐   Easy ☐

5. A woman wants to be president of the United States.

   Unrealistic ☐   Realistic ☐   Easy ☐

6. A 16-year-old girl who has just completed a driver training course wants to get her driver's license.

   Unrealistic ☐   Realistic ☐   Easy ☐

7. A gang member doesn't want to fight anymore.

   Unrealistic ☐   Realistic ☐   Easy ☐

8. A 35-year-old woman wants to compete in the Miss America pageant.

   Unrealistic ☐   Realistic ☐   Easy ☐

9. An 11-year-old boy wants to run away from home and live on his own.

Unrealistic ☐   Realistic ☐   Easy ☐

10. A straight-"A" student wants to go to college.

Unrealistic ☐   Realistic ☐   Easy ☐

Now think about your action goals. Write them down.

Three goals that are easy to accomplish:

1. _____

2. _____

3. _____

Three goals that are realistic but difficult:

1. _____

2. _____

3. _____

Do you have any unrealistic goals? If so, list them:

1. _____

2. _____

3. _____

Personal Survey

In order to set realistic goals for yourself, you need to be aware of your *strengths* and *weaknesses*. This is important to help you choose solutions (goals) that call on your strengths instead of your weaknesses.

Fill out the following personal survey by checking the appropriate box after each item that applies to you. Be honest. This is for you.

Sports	Do Very Well	Average	Do Not Do Very Well
1. Weight lifting	☐	☐	☐
2. Basketball	☐	☐	☐
3. Soccer	☐	☐	☐
4. Tennis/racquetball	☐	☐	☐
5. Track and field	☐	☐	☐
6. Football	☐	☐	☐
7. Swimming	☐	☐	☐
8. Ice/roller skating	☐	☐	☐
9. Skiing	☐	☐	☐
10. Boxing/wrestling	☐	☐	☐
11. Tumbling/gymnastics	☐	☐	☐
12. Bowling	☐	☐	☐

Skills	Do Very Well	Average	Do Not Do Very Well
1. Fixing cars	☐	☐	☐
2. Fixing mechanical objects	☐	☐	☐
3. Woodworking	☐	☐	☐
4. Sewing/needlework	☐	☐	☐
5. Gardening	☐	☐	☐
6. Cooking	☐	☐	☐
7. Photography	☐	☐	☐
8. Working with small objects/details	☐	☐	☐

School	Do Very Well	Average	Do Not Do Very Well
1. Writing	☐	☐	☐
2. Reading	☐	☐	☐
3. Math	☐	☐	☐
4. Explaining things to others	☐	☐	☐
5. Spelling	☐	☐	☐
6. Science	☐	☐	☐
7. Foreign languages	☐	☐	☐
8. Listening	☐	☐	☐

	Do Very Well	Average	Do Not Do Very Well
9. Following instructions	☐	☐	☐
10. Taking notes	☐	☐	☐

Artistic Talents

	Do Very Well	Average	Do Not Do Very Well
1. Dancing	☐	☐	☐
2. Singing	☐	☐	☐
3. Painting	☐	☐	☐
4. Sculpting	☐	☐	☐
5. Acting	☐	☐	☐
6. Playing musical instruments	☐	☐	☐
7. Designing clothes, interiors, etc.)	☐	☐	☐

Interpersonal

	Do Very Well	Average	Do Not Do Very Well
1. Keeping a secret	☐	☐	☐
2. Making friends	☐	☐	☐
3. Helping others	☐	☐	☐
4. Taking care of children	☐	☐	☐
5. Respecting others	☐	☐	☐
6. Controlling your impulses	☐	☐	☐

	Do Very Well	Average	Do Not Do Very Well
7. Compromising	☐	☐	☐
8. Sharing with others	☐	☐	☐
9. Listening/communicating	☐	☐	☐
10. Understanding others' problems	☐	☐	☐
11. Being a good team member	☐	☐	☐
12. Telling the truth	☐	☐	☐

Short-Term/Long-Term Goals

It is important to know your strengths and weaknesses so you can choose appropriate action goals. You should also understand the difference between *short-term goals* and *long-term goals*. Short-term goals can be accomplished in a brief period of time, while long-term goals may take months or years to reach.

Short-Term Goals

> Learn a new song by Friday
>
> Stick to a diet for a week
>
> Get an "A" on an assignment

Long-Term Goals

> Go to college
>
> Raise a family
>
> Write a best-selling novel

What would happen if you cared only about short-term goals? What if you cared only about long-term goals? The key is to balance your short-term and long-term goals so that a short-term goal (such as being with friends instead of doing homework) doesn't interfere with a long-term goal (such as getting into a good college or finding a good job).

Have you thought about your long-term goals? Write down some long-term goals for yourself in each of the following areas.

School:

1. _____

2. _____

3. _____

Job/career:

1. _____

2. _____

3. _____

Marriage/personal relationships:

1. _____

2. _____

3. _____

Family:

1. _____

2. _____

3. _____

Money:

1. _____

2. _____

3. _____

Self (kind of person you would like to be):

1. _____

2. _____

3. _____

Friends:

1. _____

2. _____

3. _____

Other:

1. _____

2. _____

3. _____

One of the best ways to accomplish a long-term goal is to break it down into a series of short-term goals that build up to the long-term goal. For example:

> Robert has been drinking heavily for the last 2 years. He is doing poorly in school and looks pale and thin. He has finally decided to quit drinking.

Robert's long-term goal:

> Stop drinking

Robert's short-term goals:

> Not to have any liquor today
>
> To go to a party on Friday and drink only soda
>
> To go out with his friends this weekend and pass on the beer

Write down one of your long-term goals.

_____

_____

_____

Now, break your long-term goal into three short-term goals and list them below.

1. _____

_____

2. _____

_____

3. _____

_____

Think of Solutions (Step 5)

Introduction

Once you have an idea of what you want (your goal) in a problem situation, you must then think about different responses (solutions) that will effectively meet this goal. In every case, try to think of many answers instead of limiting yourself to one. The more solutions you come up with, the more likely it is that you will then go on to make the wisest choice.

In addition to making the best choices, thinking of alternate solutions can also allow you to see things from the other person's point of view. This gives you insight into the other person's way of thinking and looking at things, and that, in turn, will make you a better problem solver.

Are your solutions usually *passive, aggressive,* or *assertive*? In this lesson you will learn about the advantages of using assertive solutions.

You will be selecting answers that put forward your own feelings, and you will be choosing those that take into account the feelings of others. You will then explore any preconceived beliefs about good and bad solutions that may *bias* your thinking about solutions. Your beliefs about things are formed from a very early age. They are created through your family, your surroundings, your friends, and your life experiences. These beliefs greatly affect any decisions you make. That is a natural part of life. But it is important to be aware of your beliefs and to know just how they can and do influence you.

Of course, before choosing a solution, you will also want to evaluate the *consequences* of each solution, particularly the costs and benefits involved. These ideas will be discussed in the next lesson.

Read each of the following problem situations carefully. Then write down as many solutions as you can. Remember, write down everything you come up with, even ideas that may seem silly or unrealistic.

PROBLEM 1: THE TICKETS

LaToya had two best friends, Lonnie and Tamika. They all liked the same rock group and were happy when LaToya's dad told her he would get three tickets for the next performance. LaToya was glad she could invite both Lonnie and Tamika because they were both good friends of hers and had done a lot of things for her in the past. However, at the last minute LaToya's dad could only get two tickets.

Write a clear definition of LaToya's problem.

_____

_____

_____

List three ways she could solve it.

1. _____

_____

2. _____

_____

3. _____

_____

PROBLEM 2: THE PARTY

Susan A. was a 19-year-old actress from a small town in Iowa. She recently arrived in California with an ambition to become a rich and famous movie star. After going to several casting agencies, she managed to land a bit part in a movie. While working on the set, she met another actress, Debbie P.

Debbie told her about a Hollywood party that night. She asked Susan to go and said they would probably meet lots of important people. Susan immediately agreed to go. At the party, Susan met a man who said he was a big movie producer. He told her that he could help her get started in her career. She was really excited until he took her aside. He scooped some white powder into a small spoon. "Here," he said. "Just breathe this in through your nose."

"No thanks," she said. "I don't need that stuff."

"Loosen up," he said. "Just trust me. You want me to help you in your career, don't you?"

Write a clear definition of Susan's problem.

_____

_____

_____

List three ways she could solve it.

1. _____

_____

2. _____

_____

3. _____

_____

PROBLEM 3: A RARE EVENT

Sondra just moved into her own apartment. It felt really good to her to be on her own at last. After she settled in, she invited her new boyfriend, David, over for dinner. She cooked a big roast and served it rare, just the way she thought meat should be served. But David never ate meat. He took one look at the roast and nearly gagged.

Write a clear definition of David's problem.

_____

_____

_____

List three ways he could solve it.

1. _____

_____

2. _____

_____

3. _____

_____

PROBLEM 4: PRIME TIME

Eric had spent the last 6 months locked up at a juvenile institution. He was really getting tired of it all—from the lack of privacy to not being able to watch his favorite TV programs. One afternoon he walked into the dayroom at his cottage, hoping to watch his favorite TV show, but another boy was watching a show Eric didn't like. The other boy seemed to be half-asleep.

Write a clear definition of Eric's problem.

_____

_____

_____

List three ways he could solve it.

1. _____

_____

2. _____

_____

3. _____

_____

Before you look at the consequences of your solutions, it is important to evaluate the type of solutions you could choose. Are your responses usually *passive, aggressive,* or *assertive?*

A *passive* person may withdraw from a situation or let others choose a goal for him or her. This person generally gives in to others and often will not protest when his or her rights are violated. Thus, while the passive person rarely hurts others, he or she suffers by not meeting his or her own needs. A passive person's self-image may be poor.

An *aggressive* person seeks self-fulfillment at the expense of others. He or she usually chooses for everyone, is very domineering, and often resorts to physical abuse to get his or her own way. An aggressive person usually does not feel good about himself or herself and takes it out on others.

An *assertive* person has a positive self-image, cares about himself or herself, and also cares about others. An assertive person speaks up, expresses honest feelings, and acts in his or her own best interests. At the same time, the person is careful not to step on other people's rights or feelings.

When you think of solutions to problems, try to focus on *assertive solutions* so you can meet your goal without hurting others. Here are some examples of passive, aggressive, and assertive responses, based on the problem situations you have just read.

PROBLEM 1: THE TICKETS

Passive LaToya: Decides it would be better not to go to the concert.

Aggressive LaToya: Demands that her dad get another ticket or simply invites one girl without regard for the other girl's feelings.

Assertive LaToya: Explains the situation to the two friends in a straightforward way. Suggests possible solutions. For example, one friend could go with her to the concert, and she would make it up to the other friend by doing something special for her later.

PROBLEM 2: THE PARTY

Passive Susan: Takes the drug and hopes the producer will help her later.

Aggressive Susan: Slaps the producer across the face and tells him to get lost.

Assertive Susan: Politely tells the producer that while she would appreciate any help he could give her in her career, she is not willing to compromise herself by taking drugs.

PROBLEM 3: A RARE EVENT

Passive David: Eats the meat, trying not to choke.

Aggressive David: Says something such as "I can't eat this gross-looking raw meat. What do you think I am, a savage?"

Assertive David: Says, "I appreciate your cooking a meal for me, Sondra. But I don't eat meat. I hope you understand."

PROBLEM 4: PRIME TIME

Passive Eric: Shrugs and mumbles to himself how nothing ever seems to go right. Walks away and goes back to his room.

Aggressive Eric: Ignores the other boy. Goes right up to the TV and puts on his program.

Assertive Eric: Goes over to the other boy and, if the boy is awake, asks nicely if he can turn the channel. He may even explain to the other boy how much he likes this show or offer him something in return.

Are you passive, aggressive, or assertive? What would be an assertive way to handle each of the following situations? Write down your ideas.

1. You are sitting in a nonsmoking section of a restaurant because smoke really bothers you. The person next to you is smoking anyway.

Your response:

_____

_____

_____

2. You are out shopping with two friends. They start shoplifting various items. Then they give you some things and tell you to take them.

Your response:

_____

_____

_____

3. In discussing the Civil War, your history teacher makes comments that you feel are offensive to your race.

Your response:

_____

_____

_____

4. You are waiting in line to buy something. Others who come after you are being waited on first.

Your response:

_____

_____

_____

Challenge Your Beliefs

Your beliefs about what is a good response and what is a bad response are learned as you grow up. You learn them from parents, friends, and teachers, as well as from other sources, such as magazines, books, and television. If you believe that a particular solution (such as talking about a problem until it's solved) is a good one, then you will be more likely to think of that solution when faced with a problem. Unfortunately, you may also believe that a solution is a good one when, in fact, it will cause harm to you or another person. In that case, you really could have chosen a less harmful solution had you first examined your beliefs.

Let's look at a few bad (and often illegal) solutions some people learn as they grow up. Each of these solutions is based on a belief that does not set a good example. After reading each belief, write two arguments against this belief, followed by a response you think would be better.

1. It's OK for a man to hit a woman if he's angry.

Two arguments against this are:

a. _____

_____

b. _____

_____

A better response would be *(complete the sentence):*

If a man is angry at a woman, he should:

_____

_____

2. If you're feeling bored, using drugs is a good way to get some excitement.

Two arguments against this are:

a. _____

_____

b. _____

_____

A better response would be *(complete the sentence)*:

If you're feeling bored:

_____

_____

3. If you want your friends to think you're OK, you have to smoke cigarettes.

Two arguments against this are:

a. _____

_____

b. _____

_____

A better response would be *(complete the sentence)*:

If you want your friends to think you're OK, you should:

_____

_____

4. If someone looks or acts different from you, you should probably beat him or her up.

Two arguments against this are:

a. _____

_____

b. _____

_____

A better response would be *(complete the sentence)*:

If someone looks or acts different from you, you should:

_____

_____

5. If a small child is screaming and won't stop, it's best to slap him or her hard.

Two arguments against this are:

a. _____

_____

b. _____

_____

A better response would be *(complete the sentence)*:

If a small child is screaming and won't stop, you should:

_____

_____

Look at Consequences (Step 6)

Introduction

While your actions undoubtedly affect you, they often affect many other people as well. Yet when you choose a particular response, do you consider the consequences of your action for both yourself *and* others? Consequences can involve *costs* and *benefits* to you and others.

What is the difference between a cost and a benefit? When an action involves bad feelings, suffering, self-denial, or deprivation, these are called the costs of an action. The benefits of an action are the opposite—positive feelings, achieving a goal, personal reward, and so forth. Do your actions usually result in more benefits than costs for you? For others?

Suppose John stays home to study for a test instead of going out with his friends.

Costs

John didn't get to go with his friends.

John probably did not have a lot of fun studying.

Benefits

John was well prepared for the test.

John probably got a good grade.

John's parents were probably happy.

Every situation involves both costs and benefits. In this lesson, you will first be asked to write down the costs and benefits of solutions to a particular problem. Then you will take a look at the consequences of crime for victims. Finally, some beliefs about the consequences of crime will be discussed.

Costs and Benefits

Read the following examples and write down all the consequences for each situation.

1. Mary has had a crush on Marcus for nearly 3 years. He never seems to notice her at all. One evening she goes to a party with her friends and sees Marcus across the room. Suddenly, he smiles at her and strides across the room to greet her. "Hi, Mary. I haven't seen you around lately," says Marcus. "Come on with me. I have some great cocaine we can share." Mary has never used drugs. If she tries the cocaine . . .

The *costs* are:

_____

_____

_____

The *benefits* are:

_____

_____

_____

What is an *alternative* solution?

_____

_____

_____

2. Lydia has saved her money to buy Christmas presents for her family. When she goes out to purchase her gifts, she finds everything costs more than she had thought, but she goes on to buy something for everyone on her list except her mother. She has no money left. She wants to buy her mother some makeup and a small

bottle of perfume. She stares at the items on display in the store and wonders if she shouldn't just take those things. If Lydia takes the makeup and perfume . . .

The *costs* are:

_____

_____

_____

The *benefits* are:

_____

_____

_____

What is an *alternative* solution?

_____

_____

_____

Pick a personal problem situation that was, or still is, difficult for you to solve. Then choose the solution you think is the *best*, writing down all the costs and benefits of doing it. After you have done this, choose the solution you think is the *worst* solution and write down the costs and benefits.

Problem situation:

_____

_____

_____

The *best solution* is:

_____

_____

_____

The *costs* are:

_____

_____

_____

The *benefits* are:

_____

_____

_____

The *worst solution* is:

_____

_____

_____

The *costs* are:

_____

_____

_____

The *benefits* are:

_____

_____

_____

**Did your best solution have more benefits or costs?
Your worst solution?**

_____

_____

_____

_____

**Did you think of costs and benefits for *others*, or did you just
write down the consequences for *you*?**

_____

_____

_____

_____

Sometimes it's hard to be aware of the consequences of your actions for others. Read each of the following situations and answer the questions that follow. (If you are doing this exercise in a group, take turns role-playing both characters in each situation. Then discuss the *consequences* for you in each role you played.)

SITUATION 1

John D. owns a small corner store. Lately, business has been very bad. To make things worse, his wife has been sick and has run up large medical bills that he is unable to pay. One morning, Mr. D. comes to his store and finds that he has been burglarized. Over $5,000 worth of merchandise has been taken—all uninsured. The police catch the burglar, an unemployed 17-year-old named Roger.

Mr. D. asks to talk to Roger. He wants to tell him about the *consequences* of burglary for a store owner.

He says:

_____

_____

_____

_____

SITUATION 2

Debra R., a 22-year-old secretary, is coming home from work late one night. As she opens her door, she is surprised by a tall figure whose face is covered by a ski mask. The man holds a knife to her throat and beats her up. Before he leaves, he makes deep slashes across her face and warns her not to call the police. But the slasher is caught and sentenced to a special rehabilitation program. This program brings assailants together with victims. At an evening therapy session, the victim begins to talk about the *consequences* of being attacked.

She says:

_____

_____

_____

_____

SITUATION 3

When Mr. J. comes home from the senior citizen's center, he is happy it is still early in the evening. He will have time to watch his favorite TV program before he goes to bed. He wants to get a good night's rest so he can be fresh in the morning. He has lots of volunteer projects in the community, and tomorrow is his favorite—building play equipment for the children at the day-care center.

As he enters his apartment, Mr. J. sees a boy ransacking his front room. "Hey," he yells. "What are you doing?" The boy is startled and makes a dash for the door. "Get out of my way, old man," he shouts as he rams Mr. J. into the wall. Mr. J. hits his head on a metal shelf. The boy runs off, and Mr. J. slumps to the floor, blood running down the side of his face.

The boy is caught by the police. If Mr. J. were to meet the boy, he would probably say:

_____

_____

_____

_____

If the children at the day-care center were to meet the boy, they would probably say:

_____

_____

_____

_____

Read the following story. It is based on a true account of a crime and its effect on the victims.

KATHLEEN'S STORY

It was a beautiful fall day, and the last thing I expected was to have anything go wrong. I had just gotten a really good grade on my history test, and I was feeling great as I rushed across the campus to play a quick game of tennis with my friend, Jan. I decided to cut through the parking garage to get to the courts. It was pretty dark in there, and it took a few moments for my eyes to adjust. Suddenly, someone grabbed me from behind and smashed me to the ground. My tennis racket skittered across the slick floor.

I started to scream, but the man held the sides of my head and bashed it over and over against the pavement. I felt myself losing consciousness as he began to slam his fists against my face and upper body. I could feel my jaw and cheekbones crush under the force of his blows. The pain was incredible, and I knew I was going to die.

I remember him pulling a knife from his back pocket. He started slashing me with it, and then he rammed it into my chest. Just then something startled him, and he jumped up and ran off. I lay there and tried to call out, but I couldn't. I kept thinking, "Why? What have I done? Who *was* that guy? Why did he attack *me*?" The next thing I knew, I was in the hospital. When I woke up, my mother was looking down at me, her eyes wide with horror.

Since that terrible day, I have had recurring nightmares about the incident. I have had numerous operations to reconstruct my face, but I will always be somewhat disfigured. People stare at me in the street. I tried to go back to school, but every time I went on campus, the whole thing came flooding back. So I finally ended up dropping out. Some of my friends came to see me in the beginning, but gradually most of them drifted off. They always wanted to go places, and I got so I hated to leave the house. I felt so ugly and hurt so much, all I wanted to do was crawl in a hole where no one could see me.

My parents were very supportive, but some of their friends seem to think that I must have been up to no good to have been involved in something like that. Maybe they think I was dealing drugs or something. Well, I can tell you, I wasn't. I've never been involved in anything like that. Maybe that guy thought I was someone else. It's kind of interesting, though. I've noticed that no one particularly wants to be around anyone who has had anything bad happen to them. I mean, it's like they shun you almost.

Since that day, my sister has been terrified to go anywhere alone. The other night she woke up screaming. My brother is mad at everyone. He can't resolve the whole thing in his mind since they never caught the man who hurt me.

Sometimes, when I least expect it, I break down in tears. Even my dad cries sometimes. I'd never seen him cry before in my life. I know it's going to take a long time to get back to normal. In fact, let's face it, our lives will never, ever be the same . . .

Your questions:

1. Who were all the victims of this crime?

_____

_____

_____

2. What were the consequences of this crime for Kathleen?

_____

_____

_____

3. Do you think the attacker thought about the effect of his crime on other people?

_____

_____

_____

4. How would the attacker have felt if the situation were reversed and someone attacked him or someone he loved?

_____

_____

_____

Note: Many months have passed since Kathleen told her story. She has joined a therapy group and thinks she may soon be able to go back to school. She would like to become a psychologist and work with victims of violence. "That way," she says, "I will use my own pain to help others overcome theirs."

Beliefs about Consequences: Errors in Thinking

Studies have shown that victimizers often distort the consequences of their actions. Sometimes they exaggerate the benefits for themselves. Other times they may blame the victim or deny the victim's suffering.

In each of the following examples, the victimizer's thinking will be pointed out. After reading the example, briefly describe what is wrong with the victimizer's thinking and what some of the real consequences of that action are.

1. Joe came home from work one day. He told his wife to leave for a few hours because his friends were coming over to play cards. She told him not to boss her around and said she was not leaving the house. "Oh, no?" he questioned, as he punched her in the face. "If you don't listen to me, I'll have to show you who's boss."

   Joe figured what he did was OK because his wife deserved what she got. In other words, he blamed his victim.

   What is *wrong* with Joe's thinking?

   _____

   _____

   _____

   Some of the *consequences* of Joe's action are:

   _____

   _____

   _____

2. Robert and Arnoldo decided to cut classes one day. They thought school was pretty boring, and they usually failed most of their classes anyway. As they were walking down the street, they saw a guy from another town coming toward them. "Hey, let's show him who controls this town," said Robert. The two boys then jumped the other guy and beat him severely.

Robert and Arnoldo thought they would feel good about themselves by showing how "tough" they were.

What is *wrong* with their thinking?

_____

_____

_____

Some of the *consequences* of what they did are:

_____

_____

_____

3. Bob was bragging to some friends about a woman he'd raped last week. One of his friends said he thought that was a terrible thing to do—that he probably really hurt the woman. "Who are you kidding?" asked Bob. "Most women like to get raped."

Bob was denying his victim's suffering.

What is *wrong* with Bob's thinking?

_____

_____

_____

Some of the *consequences* of what he did are:

_____

_____

_____

Do you think that victimizers are aware of the consequences of their actions on their victims? Have you ever been victimized? How did you feel?

Write down what happened and what you would like to say to the person who hurt you.

What happened to me was:

_____

_____

_____

_____

_____

I would like to tell the person:

_____

_____

_____

_____

_____

Lesson 10

Choose What to Do and Do It (Step 7) and Evaluate Results (Step 8)

Are You a Positive Thinker?

Answer the following questions.

Yes	No	
☐	☐	1. Do you think your life will be happy and fulfilling?
☐	☐	2. Do you feel that you are capable of controlling your life?
☐	☐	3. When you wake up each morning, do you look forward to what the day will bring?
☐	☐	4. Do you feel that you can achieve whatever you make up your mind to do?
☐	☐	5. Do you feel your goals are worthwhile?
☐	☐	6. Can you laugh at most of your mistakes?
☐	☐	7. Do you have someone with whom you share your feelings?
☐	☐	8. Do you see yourself as a winner 5 years from now?

Give yourself 2 points for each "yes" answer.

Your score _____

If you scored 12–14 points, you have a positive outlook on life; 8–10 points means you're doing OK; 6 or less means you need to improve.

One thing I could do to improve is:

_____

_____

_____

While everyone has problems, studies have shown that people who believe they are able to solve their problems are better able to cope with life, suffer less depression, and are happier than those who think otherwise.

Where do you stand? Complete the following self-survey by answering each question "T" (True) or "F" (False). Then discuss the answers with other students, friends, or family.

_____ 1. I'm capable of doing many things.

_____ 2. It's possible to handle my problems effectively.

_____ 3. I'm always getting ripped off, set up, or blamed for something I didn't do.

_____ 4. If I set a realistic goal for myself, I can almost always achieve it.

_____ 5. It's normal to have problems.

_____ 6. I have the ability to solve most of my problems.

_____ 7. I can become a better person.

_____ 8. Others are to blame for most of my problems.

_____ 9. If I fail, it's usually because I didn't try very hard to succeed.

_____ 10. If something good happens to me, it's usually because I was lucky.

_____ 11. I have a lot to be proud of.

_____ 12. People are basically good.

_____ 13. It's hard to be a teenager these days.

_____ 14. If I didn't have such a bad temper, I'd sure have
fewer problems.

_____ 15. I can learn how to be a better problem solver.

Personal Problem-Solving Review

The last two steps of effective problem solving involve choosing a response and evaluating the consequences of that response. When you evaluate consequences, you need to ask yourself if you achieved your goal without hurting yourself or others.

Now it's time to see how what you have learned fits in with your own problem-solving skills. Think about a specific problem you have faced and answer the following questions.

STEP 1: IS THERE A PROBLEM?

What was the first sign that I had a problem?

_____

_____

_____

STEP 2: STOP AND THINK

What physical reactions showed me I had a problem?

_____

_____

_____

STEP 3: WHY IS THERE A CONFLICT?

What was the specific problem?

_____

_____

_____

Did I need any more information? If so, what?

_____

_____

_____

STEP 4: WHAT DO I WANT?

What I really wanted was:

_____

_____

_____

STEP 5: THINK OF SOLUTIONS

The solution I thought of was:

_____

_____

_____

Some other solutions I could have tried are:

1. _____

2. _____

3. _____

STEP 6: LOOK AT THE CONSEQUENCES

The consequences of my solution were:

_____

_____

_____

STEP 7: CHOOSE WHAT TO DO AND DO IT

Would I have preferred a different solution?

_____

_____

_____

STEP 8: EVALUATE RESULTS

Did my solution have the effect I wanted? Was I happy with
the way I solved this problem?

_____

_____

_____

Looking Forward

In the preceding lessons you have learned to set goals and solve problems. You know that problems are a normal part of your life, and you also know you have the skills to solve most of them positively and effectively. You should see yourself as a capable person with unique talents and abilities. You can believe in yourself and in your ability to succeed.

Your success story begins today. Think. Where would you like to be:

In 5 years?

_____

_____

_____

_____

In 10 years?

_____

_____

_____

_____

Gook luck in being the best you can be!

0238